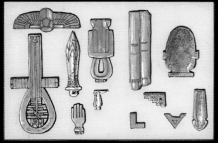

GODS & GODDESSES

IN THE DAILY LIFE OF THE

ANCIENT EGYPTIANS

Written by Henrietta McCall   Illustrated by John James

Wayland

an imprint of Hodder Children's Books

CONTENTS

INTRODUCTION

The ancient Egyptian civilization came into existence nearly 5,000 years ago. The ancient Egyptians believed that, in the beginning, the world was a dark watery chaos. Many different Creation Myths existed to explain how life began. One such story told how a giant blue lotus flower grew out of the water and, as its petals opened, sunshine flooded the world.

The temple at Heliopolis had its own version of how the first gods emerged. The story told that the first god, Atum-Ra, sneezed and spat out the god Shu and the goddess Tefnut. The children of Shu and Tefnut were Geb and Nut. Geb and Nut married each other and had four children, the gods Osiris, Isis, Seth and Nephthys. A simpler version of the creation story told that the god Ptah created all beings – the gods, humans and animals – through the thoughts in his heart and the words from his mouth.

However the world began, the ancient Egyptians believed that the world would sink back into chaos unless people behaved well and did not allow the powers of evil to take over. It was the duty of every Egyptian, with the help of the many gods and goddesses on whom he could call, to make sure that did not happen.

KHNUM
GOD OF THE NILE: RELIGION AND THE RIVER

River Nile

Desert

Desert

The River Nile was essential for the survival of the ancient Egyptians. It was their main source of water because it rarely rains in Egypt. In ancient times, the Nile rose and overflowed its banks every July, covering the land on both sides with rich black mud. The flood was called the Inundation and because it was so vital for survival it had its own gods. Khnum had power over the river. He made sure the Inundation happened every year, so that crops grew and the people did not starve.

INSIDE STORY
Khnum had a human body and the head of a ram with long curled horns. He had a great temple dedicated to him in the south of Egypt, near Aswan, on the island of Elephantine. Here, sacred rams roamed freely and when they died they were buried around the temple in stone coffins.

The two goddesses Wadjet and Nekhbet represented Upper and Lower Egypt. In this relief (right) you can see the goddess Wadjet on the left wearing the Red Crown of Lower Egypt with a cobra head-dress. Nekhbet is on the right wearing the White Crown of Upper Egypt and a vulture head-dress. The goddesses are shown on either side of the pharaoh (king), holding up their arms in protection. The pharaoh wears both the Crowns of Upper and Lower Egypt, because he was ruler of the whole land of Egypt.

FAMILY
Wife Satis
Stepdaughter Anuket

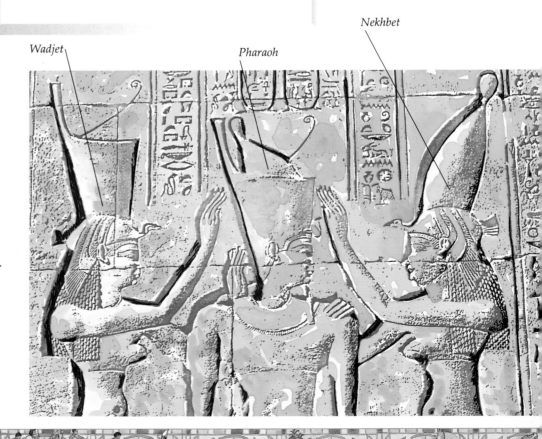

Wadjet

Pharaoh

Nekhbet

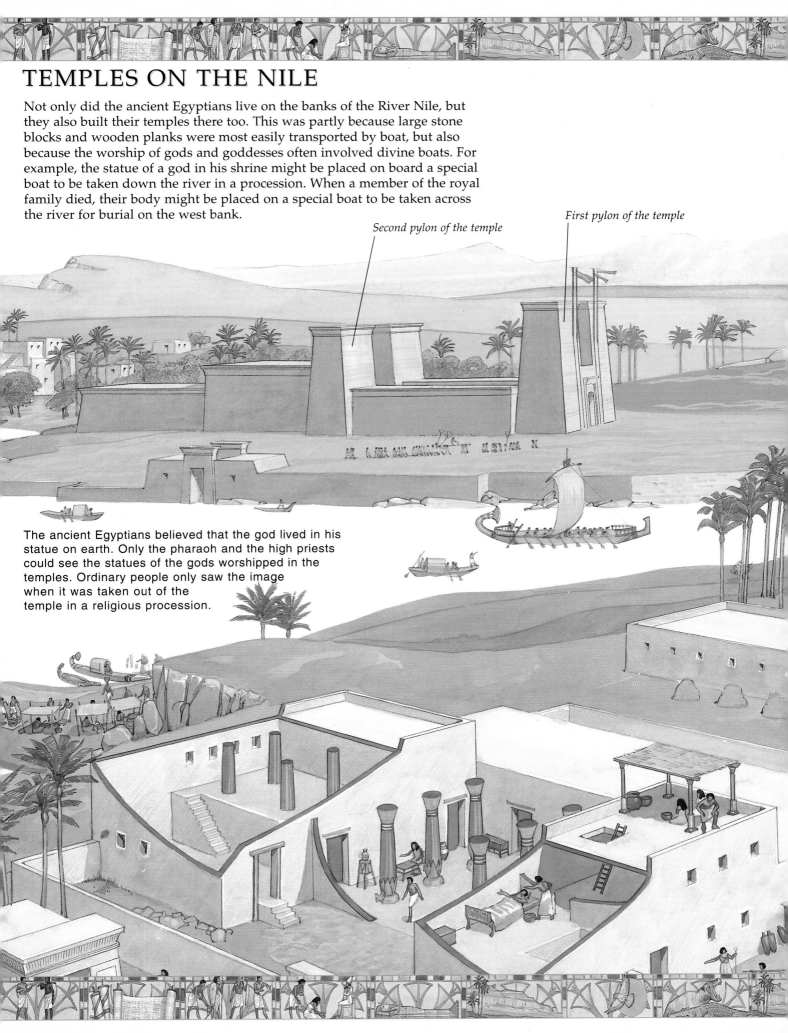

TEMPLES ON THE NILE

Not only did the ancient Egyptians live on the banks of the River Nile, but they also built their temples there too. This was partly because large stone blocks and wooden planks were most easily transported by boat, but also because the worship of gods and goddesses often involved divine boats. For example, the statue of a god in his shrine might be placed on board a special boat to be taken down the river in a procession. When a member of the royal family died, their body might be placed on a special boat to be taken across the river for burial on the west bank.

Second pylon of the temple

First pylon of the temple

The ancient Egyptians believed that the god lived in his statue on earth. Only the pharaoh and the high priests could see the statues of the gods worshipped in the temples. Ordinary people only saw the image when it was taken out of the temple in a religious procession.

RA
GOD OF THE SUN: SUN WORSHIP AND PYRAMIDS

This relief (below) shows the pharaoh Akenaten with his wife, Queen Nefertiti and three of their daughters. Until Akenaten's reign, ancient Egyptians worshipped many gods, including the great sun-god Ra. Akenaten said they must worship only one: a god called Aten, the sun disk. He changed his name to include the name of the god and he built a new capital city to glorify Aten, calling it Aketaten. In the relief, the sun disk shines down upon the royal family and from the sun radiate many beams of light which have human hands. The hands hold the hieroglyphic sign that means 'life'.

The sun was just as important as the River Nile in ancient Egypt. In one version of the sun-god legend, the ancient Egyptians believed that every morning the goddess Nut gave birth to the sun, and every night she swallowed it. During the night, the sun travelled through her body so that it could be born again the next day. The sun was worshipped as a god called Ra. He was one of the most important of all Egyptian gods.

INSIDE STORY
The sun-god Ra was usually shown as a man with a falcon's head. Above this rested a great golden sun disk. In another version of the story, Ra made his daily journey from east to west in a special sun boat, called a solar bark, which was propelled by lesser gods. The people prayed in the evening that the sun would travel safely through the dark hours. When the sun rose at dawn they praised and glorified Ra with a special hymn.

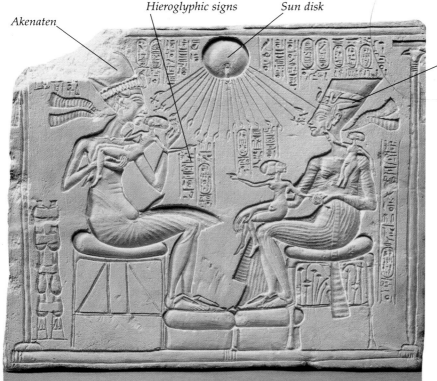

Akenaten *Hieroglyphic signs* *Sun disk* *Nefertiti*

PYRAMIDS

Pyramids are built on a square with four sides reaching to a point at the top, stretching up into the heavens to the sun god himself. Building a proper pyramid took between 20 and 30 years, so after the first few were built, the ancient Egyptians built obelisks instead. These needle-like stone monuments had pyramid-shaped points at the top. They reached just as high into the heavens as the pyramids, sometimes higher.

The body of the dead pharaoh was laid to rest in a sequence of coffins fitted inside each other, then placed in a huge stone sarcophagus. Then it was put into one of the chambers inside the pyramid. The walls of the chambers were decorated with spells which helped the spirit of the dead pharaoh make its way through the underworld and arrive safely in the afterlife. These spells are called Pyramid Texts and some of them describe the spirits of the dead sailing in the solar bark of Ra. There are about 800 spells belonging to the Pyramid Texts but no single pyramid contains them all.

HORUS
GOD OF KINGSHIP: GOVERNMENT AND ADMINISTRATION

INSIDE STORY

During the battle between Horus and Seth, one of Horus's eyes was torn out of its socket. Seth tore the eye into many pieces and dropped them into the sea. Thoth, the god of wisdom, found the pieces and put the eye together again. Horus gave the healed eye to his dead father Osiris to try and bring him back to life. The eye of Horus became a powerful symbol because it represented healing and power.

FAMILY
Father Osiris
Mother Isis
Uncle Seth

Horus was the son of Osiris and Isis and is often shown as their child, with his finger in his mouth and the side-lock symbol of youth. Horus fought and won a great battle with his dead father's wicked brother Seth. He avenged his father, the king, and so became the divine protector and god of every pharaoh. Horus was the god of kingship from even early Egyptian times. He was closely linked to the pharaoh, in whose hands the administration of the whole of Egypt was placed.

The eye of Horus (below) was one of the most common symbols in ancient Egyptian art and can be seen as a decorative device in all temples. It was a symbol of healing and power and was often used as a design for amulets, to be placed inside mummy wrappings.

Osiris

Crook

Flail

Eye of Horus

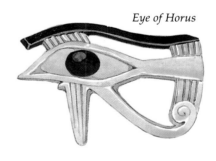

This relief (left) shows Osiris, the father of Horus, sitting on a throne in the underworld. He holds the crook and flail, symbols of kingship in ancient Egypt. The underworld was ruled by Osiris and he watched over the progress of the soul of every dead person as it passed through the underworld on its way to the afterlife.

KING AND COURT

From the very earliest times, the government of Egypt was run by a well-ordered administration. At the top was the pharaoh and under him came the Chief Vizier and other high court officials. The Chief Vizier was the man closest to the pharaoh – he knew what was happening in every corner of Egypt. Then there were the priests and the scribes, the regional governors of the provinces, and below them the mass of ordinary people, who did most of the hard labour. They built temples, palaces and ordinary houses, as well as tombs and pyramids. They reared cattle and cultivated the fields to grow food for all the people above them and for themselves. There were no slaves in ancient Egypt and the poor were looked after by the more wealthy. Nobody went hungry unless the Inundation failed.

The pharaoh wore the double crown of Upper and Lower Egypt and a false beard (right), another symbol of his kingship.

Double crown

Pharaoh

Crook

People knelt in front of the pharaoh to ask him for favours. The pharaoh also received foreigners who came to ask for his help.

Tribute

People brought gifts for the pharaoh, called tribute. The gifts included gold, jewels and rare exotic animals.

Scribe

The high court officials included the chief of the army, the chief high priest and the ambassadors who were sent to other countries as representatives of the pharaoh. They all reported directly to the Chief Vizier.

Chief Vizier   *Chief of palace guard*   *Head cook*   *Treasurer*   *Keeper of public records*   *Chief of the army*   *Priest*   *Master of the royal household*   *Fan bearer*

ISIS

WIFE OF OSIRIS: EGYPTIAN WOMEN

FAMILY
Father Geb
Mother Nut
Husband Osiris
Son Horus
Sister Nephthys
Brother-in-law Seth

Isis is one of the best known ancient Egyptian deities. Her husband was the god Osiris and her son was Horus. She was usually shown as a beautiful, slender woman in a close-fitting dress. She wore her symbol, a throne, upon her head, and sometimes had wings as well as arms. Isis had a sister called Nephthys who was very similar to Isis but sometimes appeared as a kite, a bird of prey. Like her sister, she could have wings instead of arms. When Nephthys spread her wings wide she protected shrines and coffins from evil.

Well-born Egyptian women could become priestesses, but they were not involved in the same rituals as men. At festival times, they often sang, played musical instruments (above) and danced in the temples.

Isis

Horus

This bronze and gold figurine (left) shows Isis with her baby son, Horus, on her knee. With her right hand, she cups her left breast so that the baby can drink her divine milk.

Egyptian men and women often worked together in the fields (above), cutting and harvesting the crops.

INSIDE STORY
Isis' husband Osiris was murdered by his evil brother, Seth. Isis put all the pieces of Osiris' body back together again. Nephthys had been made to marry Seth, but she was good and she helped Isis to collect the parts of Osiris' body. Isis was then able to conceive her child Horus by magic, but before she could give birth, she was captured by Seth. Isis managed to escape and Horus was born on a secret island.

WOMEN IN ANCIENT EGYPT

Although women were in some ways seen as inferior to men in ancient Egypt, they were treated well and were at the centre of family life. Egyptologists do not know if formal wedding ceremonies took place, but it is certain that the ancient Egyptians lived in family units, often with several generations living in the same house. This meant there was always someone to care for the children while the young women worked. Women laboured in the fields and orchards as well as in the home: milling wheat, making bread and preparing meals for the whole household.

Ancient Egyptian girls became mothers at what seems to us a very young age. This was because life expectancy in ancient Egypt was very short and many children did not survive beyond their teenage years. As soon as a girl was ready to bear children, her parents found her a suitable husband. Family life was considered to be good and children were considered a great blessing. Happy was the man who could boast he had several fine sons and beautiful daughters.

A family scene in a house beside the Nile (below). A young mother holds a baby on her knee while his two older brothers play with toys. The boys' hair is shaved and tied into the side-lock of youth.

OSIRIS
FIRST PHARAOH AND TAMER OF THE LAND: FARMING

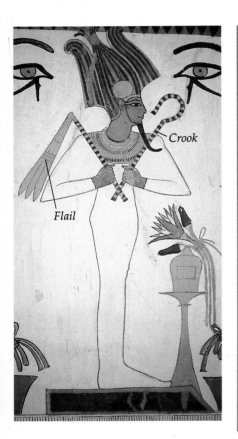

Crook

Flail

Osiris (above) was shown wearing white mummy bandages. His green face and hands represented the annual regeneration of the land after the Inundation. In his hands he held the crook and the flail, which later became symbols of kingship.

The ancient Egyptians believed that the god Osiris was the first pharaoh of Egypt. He was associated with agriculture and farming because he taught the earliest Egyptian people how to cultivate their fields. He turned the arid desert into fertile land so that crops would grow and animals could be reared.

Osiris was also the chief god of the underworld and so his image usually appears wrapped in mummy bandages.

Cattle were very important to the ancient Egyptians. They were harnessed to ploughs in the fields and in later periods were harnessed to water-wheels to raise water from the Nile for irrigation. They were slaughtered for meat and their skins used for leather. Below, a temple scribe is pictured keeping a record of how many beasts each farmer owns as they are driven past the temple steps.

FAST TRACK
Horus	p 12
Isis	p 14
Seth	p 18

INSIDE STORY
Osiris' jealous brother Seth discovered how tall Osiris was. Then he had a stone coffin made to measure. He invited 72 guests, including Osiris, to a magnificent banquet and announced that the coffin would be given to whoever fitted into it. Osiris climbed in and immediately Seth hammered down the lid and threw the coffin into the Nile. Eventually Osiris' wife, Isis, found the coffin, but before she was able to bury it, Seth retrieved the body and cut it into tiny pieces.

FOOD AND FARMING

Most people in ancient Egypt worked on the land. They grew enough food to feed everyone, from the pharaoh himself right down to the tiniest child in the most humble of homes. When the Inundation was good, there was time for two crops in one year and that meant surplus supplies could be stored ready for hard times. Grain was harvested with sickles, then threshed using oxen, winnowed and stored. Records of the quantities were carefully recorded by temple scribes.

As well as grain, the Egyptians grew lentils, vegetables and fruit. They also grew dates for eating, flavouring cakes and for making beer. There were fish to be caught from the Nile and ducks and geese from along its banks.

FAMILY	
Mother	Nut
Father	Geb
Wife	Isis
Son	Horus
Brother	Seth

A group of men are pictured (right) ploughing and sowing the land. The scribe on the right watches and records the events.

Workers divided into groups to work more effectively (below). One group stood throwing the harvested wheat up into the air so that the grain separated from the chaff. As the grain fell to the ground in a shower, other men used sticks to pile it up into heaps. The grain was then put into jars or sacks and taken away to be stored.

This figurine (left) shows what a typical farm worker wore. A simple garment made of coarse linen was wrapped around the lower body and tied at the waist. He wore no shoes or hat. Farming implements were simple – this man holds a threshing tool.

45195

SETH

WICKED GOD OF THE SKY: CRIME IN ANCIENT EGYPT

INSIDE STORY

Seth murdered his brother so his nephew, Horus, challenged him to a contest to win the crown of Egypt. The contest was to be a race in stone boats. Seth made a fine stone boat, but it was so heavy that it sank at once. Horus had been more clever. His boat was made of wood, painted to look like stone. Horus won and Seth was banished to the skies where he became the god of thunderstorms.

Seth was a wicked god. He murdered his brother, Osiris, and dismembered the body, scattering parts all over the land. Because he did this, Seth came to represent chaos, confusion and violent weather. The ancient Egyptians admired order and harmony so Seth's chaotic influence was very much feared. He usually appeared with a forked tail and cloven hooves and his monstrous head had a snout and large, pricked ears. He sometimes took the form of frightening animals such as a hippopotamus, a crocodile or a wild bull.

FAMILY

Mother Nut
Father Geb
Brother Osiris
Sister Isis
Wife Nephthys
Nephew Horus

Pictured below is the body of an ancient Egyptian peasant. There is no evidence that he was murdered; he probably died naturally. When he died, he was buried in a shallow grave in the sand, surrounded with pots and ornaments. The hot dry sand drew out the bodily fluids, leaving the skeleton covered with the skin, which eventually became hard and leathery.

Naturally preserved remains of an ancient Egyptian peasant

TOMB ROBBERY AND OTHER CRIME

If a mummy was destroyed, it meant that it could not make its journey through the underworld to the afterlife. This was why tomb robbery was considered the worst crime that an ancient Egyptian could commit. A man caught plundering a tomb might be burnt alive and one who robbed a royal tomb would be speared on a sharp stick and left to die very slowly. Nonetheless, most royal tombs were robbed during ancient times and it is not known how many robbers met this horrible end. On the whole, ancient Egyptians were law-abiding people and the most usual crime was burglary. There are many records of people stealing small objects from their neighbours. They were punished by flogging and made to return the stolen objects. Although there was no written law, there were courts of justice. Temple priests acted as judges and the courtrooms themselves were part of the temples. The results of law cases were written down by scribes and if similar cases came before the judges, they looked at what had happened before, and gave the same judgement. Punishments were usually floggings or beatings. Very seldom were criminals put to death.

Horus

Seth

This relief (left) shows Horus on the left and Seth on the right. The gods are engaged in a ritual of uniting the lotus plant of Upper Egypt and the papyrus plant of Lower Egypt. After winning the race of 'stone' boats, Horus became king of the living world, Osiris king of the underworld, and Seth was banished to the skies. However, Seth did not disappear from the order of gods. Indeed, the sun-god Ra became his champion and Seth sometimes lived with him. At night, Seth sailed with the sun-god in his sacred boat, through the hours of darkness, and kept Ra from dangerous forces.

HATHOR
GODDESS OF FESTIVITIES: MUSIC AND FEASTING

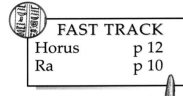
Hathor was one of the best-loved goddesses. This was because she was associated with love, festivities, music and happiness. Hathor was shown in three different ways: as a woman wearing a head-dress of a sun disk with two cow horns either side of it; as a woman with little cow ears set in a curving wig which ends with two big curls on the shoulders, or as a cow. She was the divine mother of the pharaoh and one of the ruler's royal titles was 'Son of Hathor'.

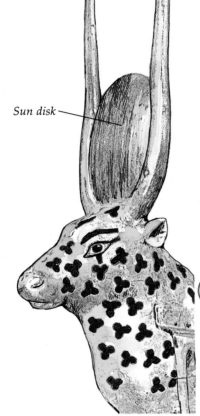

Sun disk

Above, Hathor shown as a cow. On her head was the head-dress of a sun disk with horns on either side. Sometimes when Hathor was shown this way, she also had the figure of the pharaoh kneeling beneath her belly, suckling from her udder. In this way, he was drinking her divine milk, providing him with long life and great power. In temples dedicated to Hathor, there were herds of cows considered to be sacred – their milk was kept for the pharaoh.

INSIDE STORY

Hathor also fulfilled other roles. For those who were dying, she was the goddess who would protect them on their way to the underworld. As the 'lady of turquoise' she was worshipped by those working in the turquoise mines of Sinai, in the desert. However, as the daughter of the sun-god Ra, she could assume the form of a lioness and would pounce on Ra's enemies and devour their bodies. In one Egyptian myth, she was sent to destroy all mankind.

This figure of a noblewoman (right) carries a musical instrument, symbol of Hathor, in her right hand. Her dress was made from fine linen (for which Egypt was famous throughout the ancient world). The pleats in the cloth were probably made by creasing the linen into folds, dampening it with water, then placing it between two sheets of papyrus. Then it would be trodden down and left to dry so that when it was lifted out, the pleats were set in. She also wears a wig and a circle of gold.

MUSIC

Music was very important in the daily lives of the ancient Egyptians, both in observing their religion and in having fun. There were many different types of musical instruments. Archaeologists have found the actual objects in tombs and there are many depictions of musical scenes in the reliefs and paintings found on tomb walls. There are many love poems from ancient Egypt, some of which were probably sung to a tune.

A musical instrument called a sistrum (below) was used in the worship of Hathor. When it was shaken, rather like a rattle, it produced a tinkling sound as its metal disks bounced against each other. Sistrums were usually played by high-ranking women, including priestesses, but if the pharaoh was making offerings to Hathor, he would play one too.

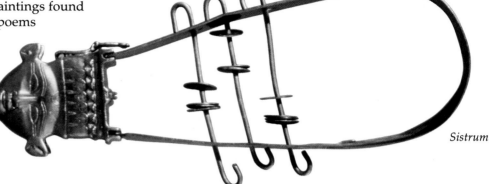

Head of Hathor

Sistrum

FAMILY
Father Ra
Stepson Horus

The handle of the sistrum was usually decorated with the head of Hathor. The eyes and eyebrows might have been inlaid with lapis-lazuli or painted with gold. Most sistrums were made of bronze.

The ancient Egyptians loved feasting, dancing and making music. As the master of the house and his wife sat on their special chairs, dancing girls and music makers entertained them. The instruments they played included pairs of ivory clappers (like castanets), harps, lutes and pipes, tambourines and trumpets. While the musicians played, they moved their bodies in time and sang.

Lyre

Harp

Wine

No Egyptian banquet would have been complete without plenty of wine and beer. They would have been brought to the feast in pottery jugs, which stood in special stands so they would not fall over.

PTAH
THE CREATOR GOD: CRAFTS

Ptah was a creator god. In the beginning he created the world and fashioned the bodies of the other gods from precious metals, especially gold. For this reason, he was the patron god of the craftsmen of ancient Egypt. Ptah was worshipped at a place in northern Egypt called Memphis. There, Ptah was the chief god and there was a great temple dedicated to him. Ptah was married to Sekhmet, a terrifying lion-headed goddess. Her name meant 'the powerful one' and she hunted the enemies of her father, Ra.

Ptah (above) is easily recognisable in tomb reliefs and paintings by his shaven head and tight skull-cap, sometimes coloured blue. His ears are left clearly visible by the cap, and he has a long straight false beard. His body is shown in mummy form, tightly bandaged, with his hands protruding in front. In his hands he holds a special staff that was the combination of three hieroglyphic signs representing power, endurance and life.

Even quite humble craftsmen such as basket-makers (above) looked to Ptah for help and protection. Baskets were made from reeds growing beside the river Nile.

This beautiful amulet (below) was found on the body of the boy-king Tutankhamun when his tomb was discovered in 1923. It is made of gold and shows Isis and her sister Nephthys on either side of a column which represents Osiris. The amulet is set with precious stones and coloured enamel and is in the shape of a shrine.

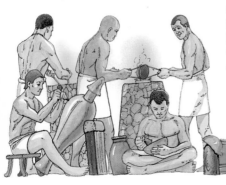

Gold was plentiful in Egypt but even so it was reserved for the king and his high officials. Craftsmen (above) were trained from an early age to cast it, fashion it, and make beautiful objects, some of which have survived undamaged to this day. Goldsmiths looked to Ptah for inspiration and help in creating their masterpieces.

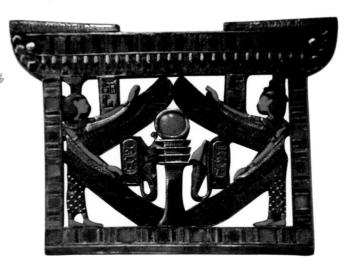

INSIDE STORY
Ptah was one of the earliest creator gods. The ancient Egyptians believed that he brought the world into existence at the beginning of time by the thoughts coming from his heart and the words coming from his tongue.

WORKING WITH WOOD

Adze

Copper blade

Copper was the first metal used in Egypt. It was made into tools, such as the blade on this adze (left), as early as the time the pyramids were built. Later on, the Egyptians used bronze, which is an alloy of copper and tin. Iron utensils and tools did not become frequent until very late in Egyptian history.

Wood was scarce in ancient Egypt. The only sources of wood in the country were palm trees, sycamore, fig, tamarisk and acacia. From earliest times, the ancient Egyptians had to go as far as the Lebanon for hard wood such as cedar, which they used to make ships. Because wood was valuable, woodworkers were carefully trained and carpentry was another skill watched over by Ptah. Archaeologists' studies of coffins and shrines show that the ancient craftsmen knew how to make skilful joins. They were also experts at putting inlays of ebony and ivory into wooden planks, as well as painting and gilding the wood.

An adze was used by woodworkers to cut away surface wood. Thick fibres of papyrus bound the copper blade to the wooden handle.

Craftsmen engaged in fine woodworking (below) enjoyed a good place in society, just beneath civil servants and people who owned their own land. They worked in special workshops to produce the objects needed by every well-to-do Egyptian, the most important of these being coffins. Without a stout and well-made coffin, an ancient Egyptian could not hope to travel safely to the afterlife.

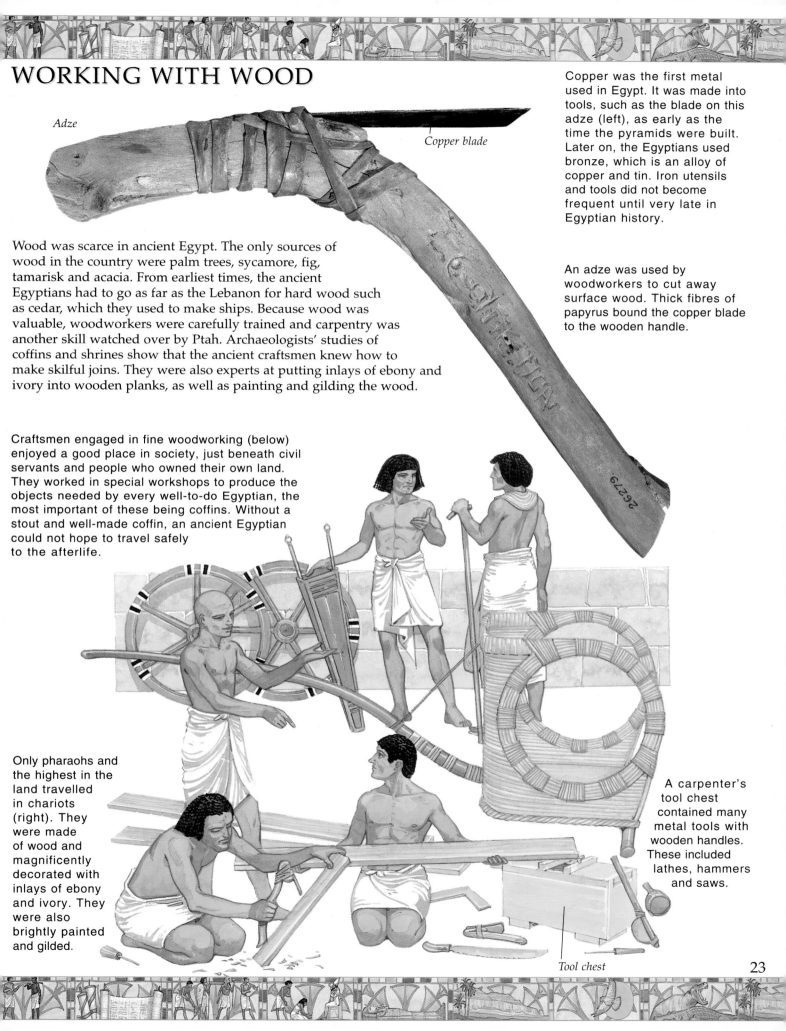

Only pharaohs and the highest in the land travelled in chariots (right). They were made of wood and magnificently decorated with inlays of ebony and ivory. They were also brightly painted and gilded.

A carpenter's tool chest contained many metal tools with wooden handles. These included lathes, hammers and saws.

Tool chest

THOTH

GOD OF WISDOM: WRITING AND SCRIBES

Thoth was the god of wisdom and writing. He was usually shown as a man with the head of an ibis bird but he could also be shown as an entire ibis or a baboon. Both creatures were sacred to him. In temples dedicated to Thoth, ibis birds were bred in captivity and thousands of them were mummified and buried in his honour. Near the greatest temple dedicated to Thoth, at Hermopolis, there is a cemetery with many mummified baboons buried in tunnels.

INSIDE STORY

Ancient Egyptians believed that Thoth kept a little book in which he wrote down the fate of every man and woman, what would happen to them and how long they would live. Some pictures and statues of Thoth show him holding a scribe's palette. He was also the keeper of secrets and a force of good magic, which he used to help the other gods.

Hieratic script – a short form of hieroglyphic script

1912
2-10
62

Egyptians wrote using hieroglyphs, picture signs which represent different letters or groups of letters. There were about 1,000 different signs and were usually written right to left. They took a long time to draw, so a short form called hieratic (left) was invented. Hieratic was mainly used for keeping records on papyrus scrolls.

This statue (left) shows Thoth as a man with the head of an ibis. He wears a pleated kilt and strides forward, his left leg in front of his right.

Thoth

THE ROLE OF THE SCRIBE

Scribes were important people in ancient Egypt. Probably even the pharaoh could not read or write and certainly most of his people could not. They relied on scribes to record everything that was important to them: for example, how much barley had been produced in the fields, or how many cows they had. Important people needed scribes to prepare the text for their tombs, describing exactly what they had achieved in life, how they had been rewarded for their services to Egypt and the details of their family. Scribes wrote on papyrus or drew directly on to stone so that stonemasons could carve out the hieroglyphic signs as directed.

This figure (right) has the hieroglyphic sign for a scribe's palette carved on his left shoulder, showing he is a scribe. Scribes are often shown with a roll of fat round the waist. This was an ancient Egyptian status symbol. It showed that the scribe had been so successful in his career that he had earned enough to overeat and put on weight. Most statues of scribes show them sitting cross-legged with an unrolled papyrus on their knees.

Bag

Reed pen

Inkwells

This scribe's palette (above) has two inkwells, one for red ink, and one for black. There is also a little bag to store the powdered charcoal used to make black ink, and a reed pen.

Carved figure of a scribe

Papyrus, which the ancient Egyptians used instead of paper, was made from a plant which grew on the banks of the Nile. The stems of the plant were harvested, tied in bundles and then made into a writing material.

First, the hard outer covering of the papyrus stems had to be peeled off. Then the stems were soaked in water so that they became soft. They were then sliced into thin strips.

The strips were beaten flat with a heavy mallet. Then they were laid in a criss-cross fashion and beaten again. A cloth was put over them and they were trampled for several days. When they had dried out, the strips formed a large flat surface ready for writing.

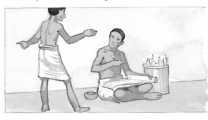

A scribe would sit cross-legged on the floor with the papyrus over his knees, writing what he was told.

BES

GOD OF FAMILY AND HEALTH: THE EGYPTIAN HOME

Bes was the protector of the home and the god of family life. He was favoured by pregnant women and women who hoped to become pregnant. In birth-houses (see page 28) his image was painted on to the walls and there are many amulets in his shape. In homes, his image might be painted on to bedroom furniture to ensure a good night's sleep and protect the sleeper from nightmares and dangerous animals.

Bes was also the god of medicine. Egyptian doctors (below) were skilled in many medical procedures. They bound wounds with linen bandages, using herbs to heal the skin and remove infection. They lanced boils and abscesses with sharp flint knives and set broken bones with splints and bandages.

A patient receiving treatment from a doctor

This statue of Bes (right) shows his high head-dress, which represented feathers. To scare away evil spirits he pulled horrible faces and stuck out his tongue.

Bes

Bes looks as if he himself is dancing, standing on one leg with the other bent up behind his body. Banging his tambourine and jumping about, he put people in a good mood.

Bes is shown holding noisy musical instruments with his arms wide apart so that he can bang them with as much force as possible. This scared off evil spirits as well as cheering people up.

People died young in ancient Egypt, though there are records of a few individuals living to a ripe old age. One pharaoh supposedly lived to well over 90. Many small children died because they were not strong enough to resist disease. Ancient Egyptian doctors had two ways of treating their patients. One way was by magic, which meant invoking spells to work a cure. The other way was by using medicines, which ranged from simple mixtures, such as honey with herbs, to more complicated treatments involving the use of crocodile teeth or other strange ingredients.

EGYPTIAN HOUSES

Houses in ancient Egypt had to take account of the very hot, dry weather. They were made from mud-bricks which were then plastered and whitewashed. White walls reflected the sun so that the houses did not become too hot inside and windows were very small to keep the house shady. Roofs were flat and in the cool of the evening, families would go up on to them to enjoy the air. The houses of richer people would have been brightly decorated inside, with painted walls and brilliantly coloured pillars. Some might have had a pool, a private chapel and beautiful gardens, watered from the River Nile. Wealthy families were waited on by many servants: cooks, maidservants, gardeners and nurses for the children.

Egyptian houses like this one (below) were rather sparsely furnished. There were beds in the bedrooms and chairs in the living areas, but most people sat on the floor on brightly coloured rugs. Chests were used to store clothes and linen as well as jewellery and sandals.

Beds were only found in the houses of rich people. Poorer people slept either on benches covered with rugs or matting, or on mats on the floor. In the daytime, the same benches could be used for the family to sit on.

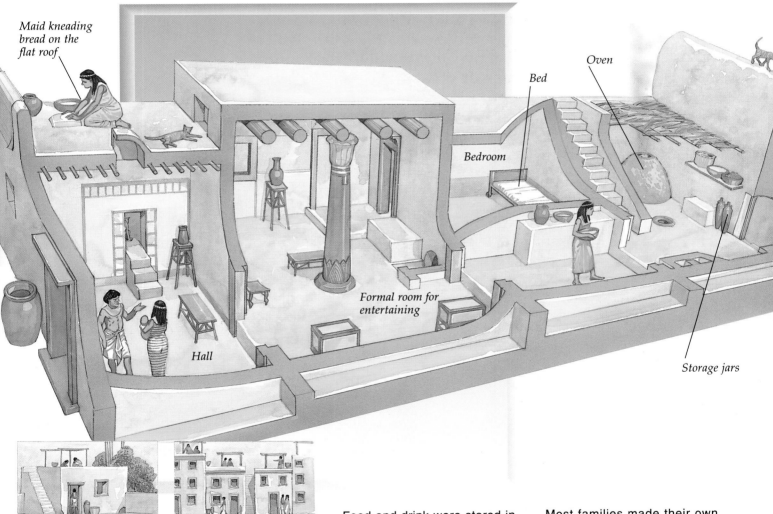

Maid kneading bread on the flat roof

Bed

Oven

Bedroom

Formal room for entertaining

Hall

Storage jars

Country houses were larger than town houses and had gardens with trees and pools. They were often set near the river to catch the cooling breeze.

In the towns and cities, houses were built much closer together and were tall and thin. There probably would have been a small yard.

Food and drink were stored in pottery jars. Those which stored grain had wide necks and those that stored oil or wine had spouts. Dates and some vegetables such as onions were stored in large baskets. But fresh food did not last well in such a hot climate so it was eaten as soon as possible.

Most families made their own beer, wine and bread. Bread was baked in a clay oven which was heated with wood and scrub. Meat, including fowl such as duck, was roasted inside the oven. Cooking in a big house or palace would have been done by specially trained servants. Families ate together, using their fingers.

TAWARET

PROTECTOR OF PREGNANT WOMEN: CHILDREN

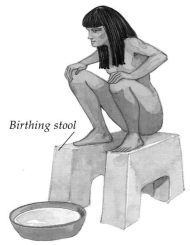

Birthing stool

Egyptian women were taken to a special birth-house when they were ready to give birth. They often gave birth squatting on a birthing stool. A female relation or midwife held the baby as it was born.

Poor women breast-fed their babies themselves. Richer women paid other women who had just given birth to feed their baby as well. Eventually, the baby was taken away from the nursing-mother and went back to its real parent.

The pharaoh is pictured (right) surrounded by his family – his queen and two children. Every ruler wanted fine sons as heirs to the throne.

Tawaret provided divine protection for women in childbirth. She was a mixture of several creatures, having the head and body of a hippopotamus, a lion's paws and a crocodile's tail. All these parts from such fierce animals gave her great strength. Nonetheless she was a good goddess and her fierceness was only directed against those who threatened the people she protected. Tawaret also had breasts and a round belly, revealing her association with pregnant women.

Tawaret

Young children had a special hairstyle called 'the side-lock of youth', as on these two boys below. All their hair was shaved off except for a long lock of hair which hung down one side of their head.

Royal family

Pharaoh

Queen

Side-lock of youth

Toy

INSIDE STORY

Tawaret was one of the wives of the wicked god Seth. In one story, Seth turned himself into a bull and stamped on his brother Osiris until he was dead. As a punishment, the gods cut off one of the bull's legs and cast it to the heavens where it appeared as a star. It was Tawaret's duty to guard the foreleg and ensure it never left the heavens to harm anyone again.

CHILDREN

Bearing children, especially fine sons, was the duty of every Egyptian woman, from the queen down to the humblest peasant. Because so many children died in infancy, it was important to produce as many as possible to replace those that died. Every couple hoped their children would look after them in their old age. Sons worked in the fields while daughters-in-law and unmarried daughters ran the home. Ancient Egyptian children were not banished to their own quarters but lived very much in the centre of the family, sharing meals with their parents and probably sleeping in the same room. In richer houses they had their own rooms and were looked after by their own servants. They were expected to respect their parents and to do what they were told.

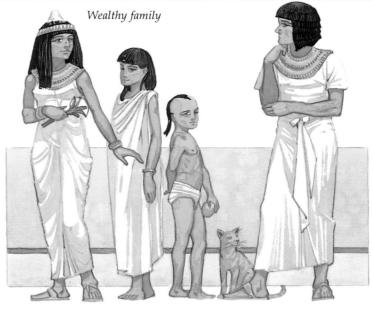

Wealthy family

Court official and his wife

In the houses of the rich, children were often dressed in the same way as their parents. Young children wore nothing, or just a linen loincloth (above).

Egyptian children, rich and poor, had pets (above). Dogs and cats were much valued. Richer children had more exotic pets such as monkeys or gazelles.

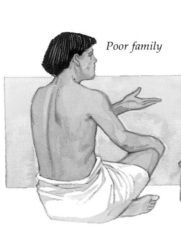

Poor family

This little wooden horse (left) has wheels so it can be pulled along on a string. Other toys included board games, balls and dolls, some with moving arms and legs.

In the houses of poorer people (above), young children ran around naked. The father spent most of the daylight hours working in the fields while the mother ran the house, making sure there was a good meal for her husband when he came home.

Toy horse

ANUBIS
GOD OF EMBALMING: MUMMIES

Anubis is pictured above leading a soul to judgement. Anubis was a powerful god and his image appeared on all the sealed doors of burial chambers. Tomb robbers knew that if they broke the seal, the god would take his revenge.

Anubis was the chief god of the dead. The Egyptians believed that Anubis had invented the process of mummification and that he watched over the men who mummified the bodies of dead Egyptians. Anubis was shown as an all-black jackal-type figure or as a human figure with the head of a jackal. His ears were always pricked and pointed. When embalmers were at their work, they sometimes wore Anubis masks.

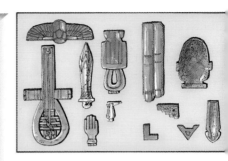

Small objects called amulets (above) were placed among the folds in a mummy's bandages. One of the most important amulets was the heart scarab, which was placed directly over the place where the heart had once been. Many were in the shape of gods or gods' symbols and some were in the shape of divine animals.

Once the pharaoh's body was laid in the bottom half of his mummy case, the top half could be put in place (below). The two parts were sealed tight with pitch, a sticky glue that held the case together so that it would never come apart. It had to be secure to make its hazardous journey through the underworld.

This mummy case is beautifully decorated with all the attributes of kingship: the wig with twin cobras, the false beard and the crook and flail held in crossed hands.

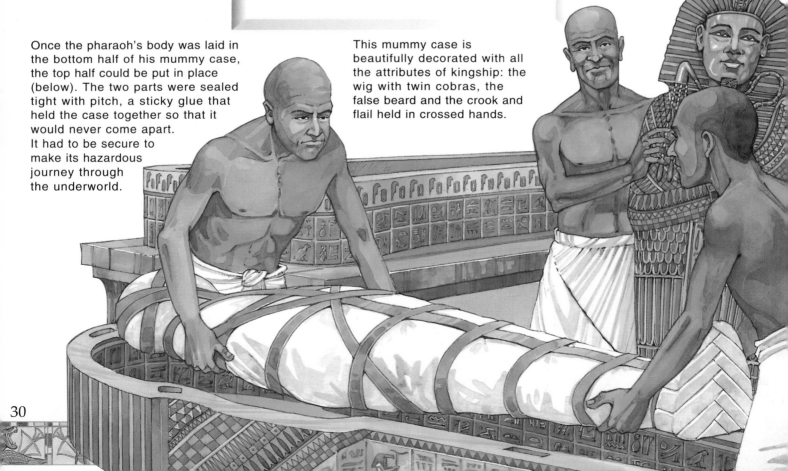

MUMMIFICATION

The ancient Egyptians invented the process of mummification. They believed that in order to survive in the afterlife, a body must arrive there in as lifelike a state as possible. To do this, they had to make sure it did not rot, something that would have happened very quickly in a hot country like Egypt. Immediately the person died, he was removed to the embalmers' workshop. The internal organs were removed and placed in special jars called 'canopic jars'. Then the body was thoroughly washed before being placed in a bath of natron salts which dried it out until the skin looked rather like leather. After 70 days, the body came back to the embalmers' workshop. Because the natron had dried out the body so much, the skin of the body was hard and had to be rubbed with oil to make it supple again. The spaces in the body where the internal organs had been were padded out with straw or folded linen. The embalmers tried to make the body look like it had in its lifetime.

INSIDE STORY
Anubis had several special names. One was 'lord of the sacred land' which referred to his role as master of the burial ground. Another was 'foremost of the divine booth', meaning Anubis was the most important figure in the embalmers' workshop.

This mummy and case (right) belonged to a high-ranking woman of status. In early times, the portrait on a mummy case did not look like the person inside, but later on, attempts were made to present a true portrait of the individual.

Sometimes garlands of flowers were placed over the bandaged mummified body and sweet-scented oils poured over it before the top half of the case was securely fixed.

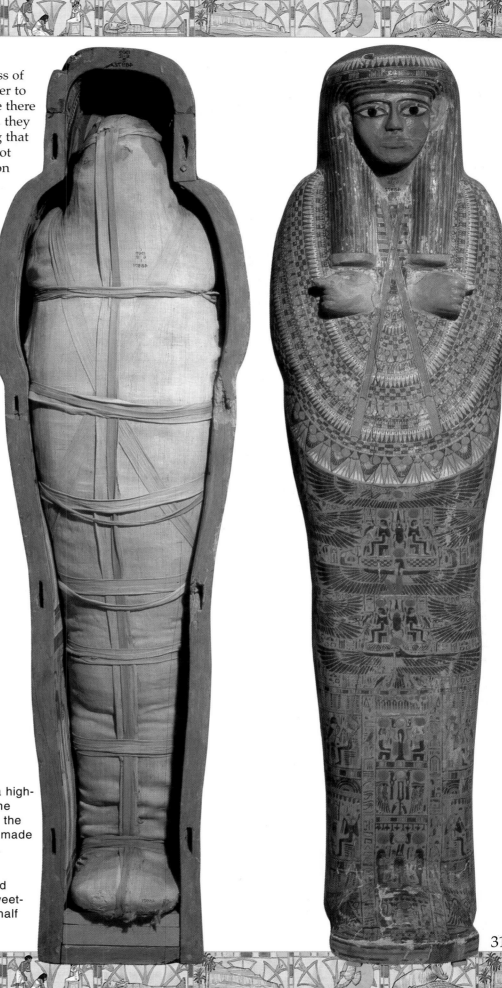

31

MA'AT
GODDESS OF TRUTH: THE WEIGHING OF THE HEART

In the weighing of the heart ceremony (below), Ma'at stood beside the balance. In one scale pan was the heart of the dead person, in the other Ma'at's feather of truth. Anubis knelt beneath the balance. Beyond it Thoth, wearing his ibis head, kept a record of the dead person's actions.

Ma'at was the goddess of truth, justice and order. She was portrayed as a woman with a feather on her head and sometimes wore a dress patterned with feathers. Ma'at was the goddess who made sure the seasons changed, that the stars moved in the heavens and that gods and humans were in harmony. Ma'at was also the patron goddess of judges. They wore an image of her as part of their uniform.

INSIDE STORY
When an ancient Egyptian died, his mummified body and his soul went on a long, dangerous journey through the underworld. They would meet monsters and demons and have to overcome them. In the Hall of the Double Ma'at the heart of the mummy was weighed against the feather of Ma'at. This meant that the thoughts and actions of that person in life were measured against absolute truth and justice. If the person failed the test, they would remain in the underworld and not pass through to the afterlife.

Weighing of the heart ceremony

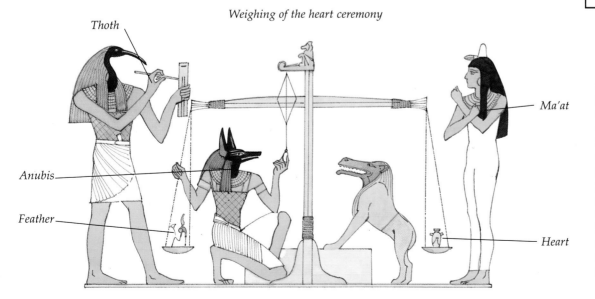

Thoth

Anubis

Feather

Ma'at

Heart

On the walls of the Hall of the Double Ma'at, in the underworld, were written verses from the Book of the Dead (see right). This was a collection of magic spells to help the dead person give the right answers when he was asked questions. He had to know, for example, the exact names of the monsters and demons that he might meet.

THE AFTERLIFE

The ancient Egyptians were not obsessed with death. They enjoyed their lives on earth so much that they wanted to ensure that after they died they would be even happier in the afterlife. So they spent much time preparing for their own deaths and looking after their relatives who had already died. A mummified body was placed in its tomb with many objects that it might need on its journey to the afterlife. These included weapons, clothes, jewellery, food and drink. Pharaohs were even provided with boats.

The mummified body was taken to the tomb in its case with the objects which were to be buried with it. The mummy case was propped up against a wall while a family member 'opened' the mouth and nose using a special instrument (right). A priest dressed like the god Anubis watched over the ceremony.

Opening of the mouth ceremony

Priest

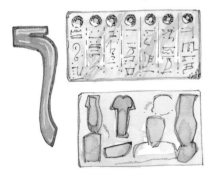

Instruments for the opening of the mouth ceremony

In rich burials, many different tools were used for the opening of the mouth ceremony (left). It was necessary to open various different parts of the body, (ears, eyes, nose etc) and there were special instruments for doing this. Most of the tools were made of sharpened stone or metal.

Shabtis

Every tomb contained a number of little servant statues, called *shabtis*, which were there to do the work and miraculously came to life when they were needed. They were often kept together in a special wooden chest (left). The name and details of the dead person were recorded on the outside of the chest. The shabtis themselves looked like tiny mummies.

THE BOOK OF THE DEAD

The Book of the Dead contained 190 spells. One of the most important was number 125, called the Negative Confession. A long list of wrong-doings was read to the dead person and he was asked if he had done any of them. If he could truthfully answer "No" to them all and then passed the weighing of the heart ceremony, he became a blessed spirit. Using another spell from the Book of the Dead, he could then turn himself into a bird. This enabled him to fly up to the living world during daylight hours and visit the people he loved.

A M U N
KING OF THE GODS: KARNAK TEMPLE

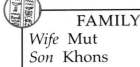

FAMILY
Wife Mut
Son Khons

Amun is one of the greatest gods of the Egyptian pantheon. By the time of the New Kingdom, he was the King of the Gods and his most important temple, at Karnak, became the richest in the land. He was believed to have joined forces with the sun-god Ra, and was sometimes called Amun-Ra. Although he was so mighty, Amun was also kind and understanding. He was a mysterious god and his name meant 'the hidden one'.

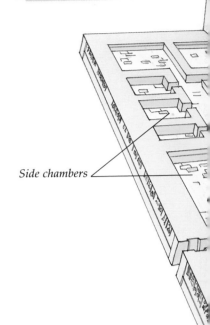

Side chambers

Amun was easy to recognise because of his crown, which consisted of a sun disk with two huge feathers at the top (above). He also wore a false beard and his skin was sometimes painted the colour of the midday sky. Sometimes he appeared as a ram with short curved horns.

The entrance to the great temple at Karnak was approached by a processional way, guarded on both sides by a row of sphinxes. Usually sphinxes were lions with human heads. At Karnak, they were lions with ram heads (below) because the short horned ram was sacred to the god Amun.

INSIDE STORY
Even though Amun was so mighty, he was also compassionate to the poor and weak. There was a special prayer to him: "Amun knows how to be kind and hears anyone who cries out to him". Because of this merciful side to his character, Amun became a very popular god and was even worshipped beyond the borders of ancient Egypt.

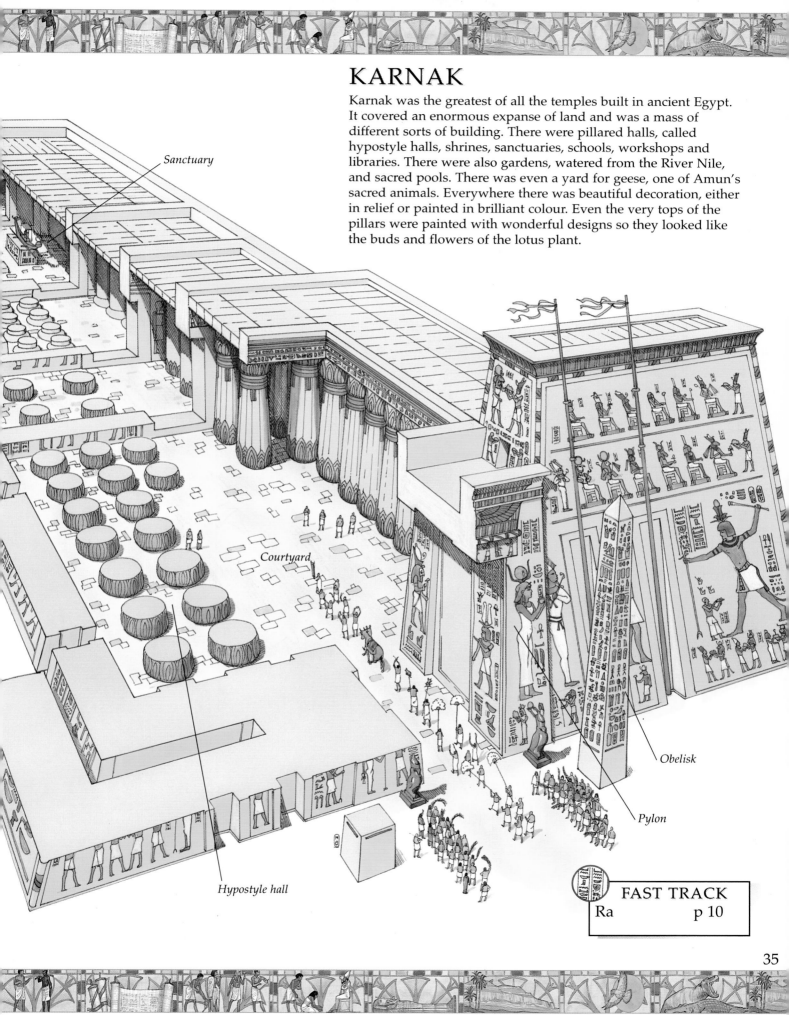

KARNAK

Karnak was the greatest of all the temples built in ancient Egypt. It covered an enormous expanse of land and was a mass of different sorts of building. There were pillared halls, called hypostyle halls, shrines, sanctuaries, schools, workshops and libraries. There were also gardens, watered from the River Nile, and sacred pools. There was even a yard for geese, one of Amun's sacred animals. Everywhere there was beautiful decoration, either in relief or painted in brilliant colour. Even the very tops of the pillars were painted with wonderful designs so they looked like the buds and flowers of the lotus plant.

Sanctuary

Courtyard

Obelisk

Pylon

Hypostyle hall

FAST TRACK
Ra   p 10

PHARAOHS
WORSHIPPED AS GODS

Occasionally human beings were worshipped as well as gods. Usually these were very powerful pharaohs who decreed that they should be worshipped as gods. Two such rulers were Ramesses II and the great queen Hatshepsut. It was rare for an ordinary person to become a god, but one who did was the architect Imhotep. Two thousand years after his death, he was made a god and worshipped for his wisdom.

Temple at Abu Simbel

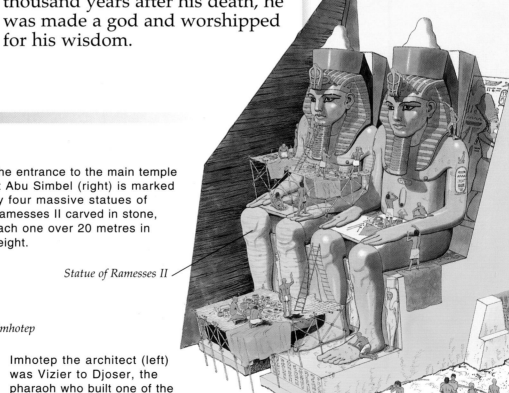

The entrance to the main temple at Abu Simbel (right) is marked by four massive statues of Ramesses II carved in stone, each one over 20 metres in height.

Statue of Ramesses II

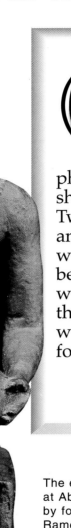

— *Imhotep*

Imhotep the architect (left) was Vizier to Djoser, the pharaoh who built one of the earliest pyramids, the Step Pyramid at Saqqara. In his own lifetime, Imhotep was an important man but not a god. It was not until later times that he began to be worshipped as a god skilled in wisdom and medicine. Some people believed that his father was Ptah.

ABU SIMBEL

The place of Ramesses II's greatest monument to himself was at the First Cataract at a place called Abu Simbel. There, overlooking the Nile, Ramesses built two wonderful temples to himself and his royal wife Nefertari. Inside his temple are carved scenes of his great victories in Nubia to the south and over the warlike Hittite people to the east. At the very back of the temple, Ramesses is shown as a god along with the true gods Ra, Ptah and Amun. The smaller temple is Nefertari's and is dedicated to the goddess Hathor. Even though Nefertari was his chief royal wife, she was not made into a goddess in her own right. The temple at Abu Simbel is one of the most impressive monuments that survives from the ancient Egyptian civilization.

Hatshepsut wanted to show she was just as powerful as a male pharaoh. She had herself depicted wearing a kilt and a false beard (left).

An epic poem celebrating Ramesses' military strength was written in hieroglyphs and decorated the temple walls.

Four statues of seated figures were placed in the inner sanctum. They represented Ramesses with Ra, the sun-god, on his left and Amun and Ptah on his right.

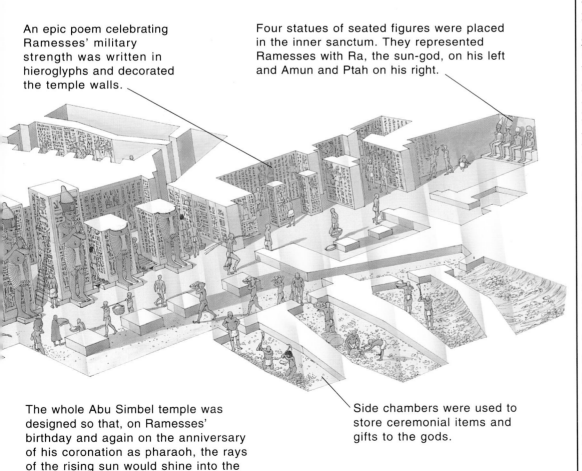

The whole Abu Simbel temple was designed so that, on Ramesses' birthday and again on the anniversary of his coronation as pharaoh, the rays of the rising sun would shine into the temple, lighting up the statues at the back of the inner sanctum.

Side chambers were used to store ceremonial items and gifts to the gods.

INSIDE STORY

Ramesses II was not really royal at all – his grandfather had only been a high court official who had taken over as ruler when the old pharaoh died and there was nobody to succeed him. Ramesses I only reigned for a very short time, after which his ambitious son took over the throne. Ramesses II proceeded to turn Egypt into a major world power with a vast empire stretching to the far south and the east. Whenever Ramesses II won a battle he commemorated it by setting up a large stone tablet describing the wonderful victory and he poured glory on himself for all his great works.

WORSHIP
PEOPLE, PRIESTS AND TEMPLES

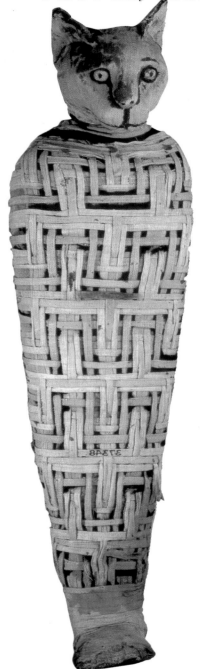

Religion was an essential part of everyday life in ancient Egypt. The most important gods and goddesses had their own temples and cults. Priests made daily offerings and said prayers in front of a statue or an animal which was thought to be the earthly body of the god, for example, a cow for the goddess Hathor. The people believed that if they were honest and behaved kindly towards others, the gods and goddesses would be happy.

PRIESTS

There were several different sorts of priests in ancient Egypt but they were all expected to live in the temple when they were on duty. They also had to be pure. That meant living apart from their wives and not eating food which was considered unclean, such as fish. Some priests were allowed to copy out holy spells, and some to observe the stars and make astrological predictions.

This is a mummy of the cat-goddess Bastet (above). In later periods she was worshipped by women who wanted to have a child. In her temple, there were hundreds of sacred cats running about. When they died they were mummified, keeping the cat shape of the body and wearing a cat mask.

Every city's temple was guarded by a massive gate called a pylon. Sometimes there were two pylons, one behind the other.

Once past the pylon, visitors found themselves in an enormous courtyard which contained pillars and colossal statues of gods and kings. There might also have been obelisks, tall, slender needles of stone that seemed to touch the roof of the sky because they reached so high.

Temple entrance

Pylon

Obelisk

THE PEOPLE AND THEIR GODS

An Egyptian man or woman would have selected a particular god or goddess to be his or her own special patron. For example, a craftsman, working in wood, stone or precious metals, might have chosen Ptah and made special offerings to him. Scribes chose Thoth as he was the god of knowledge and writing. And the dead were thought to pray to the god of the underworld Anubis, to ensure a safe passage through the darkness before they arrived in the afterlife.

The temple in an ancient Egyptian city was at the centre of everyday life. Although an ordinary Egyptian could only go into the temple's courtyards, he believed that the god in his sanctuary was looking after him and could see and hear everything that was going on all around. Temples were built of stone and were beautifully decorated because every temple was a god's home. In the sanctuary, the statue of the god was looked after by high priests. It was fed and washed and clothed by them. On high days and holidays, the image of the god was taken out and transported through the city on a special palanquin so that ordinary people could see and worship him.

CELEBRATION

AND DESPAIR: THE INUNDATION

All through the year there were festivals and celebrations because the ancient Egyptians enjoyed having a good time. It was only at times of national emergency, such as when the Inundation failed, that they did not celebrate the annual festivals. The failure of the Inundation caused severe hardship for all of Egypt. Without the flood and the rich mud it left behind, the land could not support crops and left animals and people starving.

This fragment (above) shows Hapy, god of the Inundation. The breasts represented fertility, as did his round belly which was rather like that of a pregnant woman.

The Nilometer (above) is the name of a device the ancient Egyptians used to measure the level of the Nile. A check was regularly kept as to which step the river was up to. At the time of the Inundation scribes were able to record how quickly the water was rising by measuring how many steps had been covered. Records of the height of the Inundation were kept for years and scribes used these to try to predict how high the river would rise every year.

This photograph (right), taken from the air, clearly shows the line between the fertile watered land and the arid desert. Nowadays, the Nile is contained by the High Dam at Aswan, so the flow of water to the land is regular and constant. There are no more Inundations.

THE SED FESTIVAL

One of the most important events was the sed festival which pharaohs celebrated after they had been reigning for 30 years. The people came to pay homage to the pharaoh as he sat in a special pavilion. After the ceremonies were complete, the pharaoh went on a ritual race, running between boundary markers which were meant to represent the boundaries of Egypt. As some pharaohs must have been quite old by the time they had reigned for 30 years, they sometimes celebrated their sed festival a little early.

FAST TRACK
Anubis   p 30
Festivals   p 42

The ceremonies were closely watched by high court officials and priests within the pavilion. Ordinary people no doubt watched the running race as well, but probably from further away.

INSIDE STORY
Just as Lower and Upper Egypt had their own symbolic crowns, so the two regions were represented by different plants: the papyrus plant for Lower Egypt and the lotus plant for Upper Egypt. Hapy is often portrayed with both of these plants to show that he was responsible for the fertility of the whole land. Aquatic plants sometimes also decorated his head-dress, including reeds, water-lilies and bullrushes.

The White Crown worn by the pharaoh symbolised Upper Egypt and the Red Crown, Lower Egypt. Pharaohs often wore both at once, the White Crown inside the Red Crown to symbolise the unification of the two lands. No crowns have ever been unearthed from ancient Egypt. They were probably made of linen stretched over a wooden frame.

The sed festival takes its name from a god called Sed who was rather like Anubis in appearance, with a jackal's head. Apart from his connection with the royal jubilee, Egyptologists know nothing of this god and he seems only to have been known through this festival. Sometimes the festival went on to celebrate the cult of a dead pharaoh. A god of the underworld such as Sed would have been important to look after Egypt's ruler on his journey to the afterlife.

FESTIVALS

INSIDE STORY

The Festival of Opet was one of the most important festivals in the ancient Egyptian calendar and it probably lasted about three weeks during the period of the Inundation. During the festival, the divine image of the god Amun went in procession from his temple at Karnak to the temple at Luxor, both of which are on the east bank of the Nile at Thebes. The processional route was lined by sphinxes. The festival celebrated the divine marriage between the mother of the pharaoh and Amun. After the marriage, the pharaoh would enter the temple sanctuary and after solemn rites were performed, he would come out again as a god.

The ancient Egyptians celebrated and held festivals throughout the year. Fifty-four annual festivals have been found listed on the walls of Pharaoh Tuthmosis III's temple and Ramesses III (right) had 60 in his. The most common type of festivals took place when a god or goddess's statue was taken from one temple to be placed in another. People lined the route between the two temples and worshipped and glorified the divine image as it passed along the way.

This sarcophagus lid portrays Ramesses III as a mummy, with the goddesses Isis and Nephthys on either side of him.

BEAUTIFUL FESTIVAL OF THE VALLEY

The Beautiful Festival of the Valley took place at Thebes. The holy family of Thebes – Amun, his wife Mut and his son Khons – were taken from the temple at Karnak to the temple at Deir el-Bahri, which was across the Nile. The statues were carried inside shrines on divine barks down to beautiful boats moored at the river's edge. Once across the river, the holy family's statues were carried carefully up to the temple. All along the route, ordinary Egyptians were allowed to watch the wonderful procession and they bowed down as the deities passed by.

Sphinxes protected the statue of a god as it passed on its way from one temple to another. A sphinx was a mythical beast with the head of a human on the body of a lion. This gave the monster the most powerful brain allied to the most powerful body. Egyptian sphinxes nearly always appeared in pairs and quite often in avenues, in which case the sphinxes were placed staring at one another across a road or path. At certain places along the sphinx avenue were bark stations, where the heavy weight could be rested before being carried once more on its way.

Priests were in charge of the religious festival taking the gods across the river. It needed many strong young men to carry a heavy stone statue of a god in a sacred bark on poles (below). These barks were similar to ordinary Nile boats but, instead of a cabin, there was a shrine in which the statue was placed for the journey. Wonderful fans made of ostrich feathers attached to long poles fluttered in the breeze and added to the colourful procession.

GLOSSARY

Amulet A small figurine or charm believed to bring luck or to protect the wearer from harm.

Bark A special type of boat used to transport statues of gods from one shrine or temple to another. They were also called sacred barks.

Egyptologist A person who studies the history and language of the people of ancient Egypt.

Hieratic A shortened form of hieroglyphs which were quicker and easier to write.

Hieroglyph The ancient Egyptian form of writing, mainly carved onto monuments.

Hypostyle A contruction having a roof supported by pillars.

Lapis-lazuli A semi-precious dark blue stone, flecked with gold, used in ancient Egyptian jewellery.

Natron A form of natural salt used for drying out a body during the mummification process.

New Kingdom The history of Egypt is divided into three main sections: the Old Kingdom (2575-2134 BC, when the pyramids were built); the Middle Kingdom (2040-1640 BC), and the New Kingdom (1550-1070 BC, when Egypt flourished as a major world power).

Palanquin A light structure of painted and decorated wood used to house the statue of a god while it was being carried on a bark.

Pantheon The collection of all the gods and goddesses of ancient Egypt.

Papyrus A plant which grew along the banks of the Nile. Its image appeared as decoration all over ancient Egypt and it was also used to make boats, sandals ad ropes. It was pressed into flat sheets for writing on.

Pharaoh The name for the king in ancient Egypt. The word actually means 'great house', referring to the palace where the ruler lived.

Pylon The great gate or entrance to an Egyptian temple, made up of two towers and a great doorway between them.

Sanctuary Holy place, often the innermost part of a temple.

Sarcophagus A large outer coffin, usually made of stone.

Scarab A model of a dung beetle. The most commonly used amulet in ancient Egypt was shaped as a scarab.

Shabti A little figurine which the ancient Egyptians believed came to life in the underworld. Rich people could be buried with over 200 shabtis.

Side-lock of youth The long lock of hair left on the side of a child's head when the rest was shaved off.

Tribute Taxes paid in goods to Egypt from other conquered lands. Goods such as gold, silver and semi-precious stones were also given to Egypt as gifts, or tribute, from foreign lands.

Winnow To separate the chaff from the grain when harvesting wheat or barley.

INDEX